Love Is On The Front Line:

A STORY OF HOPE

ROXIE BERRY

ISBN: 979-8-9902680-6-7

Publishing By: DemiCo National, LLC

www.DemiCoNational.com

4

Thank You

Thank you,

For your word of wisdom and knowledge.

Thank you,

For always putting a smile on my face.

Thank you,

For Hearing me out and never showing me a cold shoulder.

Thank you,

For being you. It is like you can read my mind or something if I feel down in the dumps.

Thank you,

For coming to my rescue and always lending a helping hand.

Thank you,

For never being ashamed, showing gratitude and appreciation.

Thank you,

For believing in me when I could not believe in myself.

Thank you,

   For being unique in your own distinct way.

Thank you,

For encouraging words, it goes a long way.

Thank you,

For the long-lasting friendship that means a lot.

Heart to heart.

Fuel & Fire

F: For every test that I have been in.

U: Understanding that the test was in place to teach me a lesson.

E: Even though it was difficult grasping what I needed to learn, I eventually caught on.

L: Letting what I have learned change me was the best thing that could have happened to me.

F: Familiarizing myself with the new me was quite a challenge because I was content with my old self.

I: I decided to fully embrace my new life despite the times I wanted to turn back around.

R: "Really" is what I would say to myself when I wanted to turn back. I am glad I decided to see what this new self would bring.

E: Every day has not been rainbows with the new me. However, it is more of a drizzle instead of a hailstorm. I can deal with that.

Life & Love

Nine months is how long it takes for a life to be created. Unfortunately, it can be taken away in a matter of two seconds. Cherish the time you have alive because we all must die one day. While you can take another breath, step into your calling, and take over the world. Your life is an example for someone to express what joy, peace and even riches look like. Do not take your life for granted. Not even for a second because were created for a reason. It is up to you to find out what that reason is. It is time to soar and allow your life to produce grandiose things. What dream have you put down because of the thoughts of not being good enough? I am here to tell you that you are good enough. Now pick it back up. It is okay to start over, do not quit. If you quit, you will wish you were where you are now. It will all fall in place just do not give up!

Teardrops

If teardrops could speak, they would tell the hated story you kept on the inside for a long time. Teardrops fall so swiftly but are like heavy stones. I understand not being able to have the right words to form a sentence because of how heavy things can get. The difficulties of life can be hard. Bottling up everything will cause things to overflow and be expressed through words, your actions, or even your tears. If your tears could fill a space and tell a story you could not explain, I am sure it would equate to a pond. A pond that is filled with anger, anxiety, fear, depression, confusion, and even sorrow. If you must, cry, because sometimes crying is the only way that we can release what we have had bottled up on the inside. Do not allow the tears that fall to keep you hidden from what could be. Eventually, you will see that your teardrops were watering the seeds you planted throughout the years to form a beautiful outcome. Keep going and allow yourself to understand that even though my tears fall and may be heavy like stones, it will all work together.

Nourishment

What gives you nourishment? As water gives life to plants and love cures the brokenhearted, everything that is nurtured properly will live. If you want something to grow and become good, you will take care of it but if you neglect something it will be sure to die. So, take care of those things. The plans that you have, the life that you want to live, and the love that you want to give and receive you must give life to. Sometimes we can briefly take care of something and then stop because it appears to be growing. We think that it is being well nourished, but little do we know it is really dying on the inside from being malnourished. Remember, if you want a good result, you must tend to it with good things. If you want a good mind, you must feed it positive words. If you want a good body, you must tend to it with healthy food and exercise. If you want a good plant, you must tend to it with water and soil. What have you allowed to go malnourished because you did not take care of it with good intentions?

Milestone

What is a milestone you say? A milestone is when you reach a point in life that was significant for you. We all have milestones that we want to reach. We may have to go through a few things, but they can be reached, and we can get there. The milestones and goals will always be there unless you choose to not reach for them. Have there been any goals that you wanted to work towards, but you gave up on? My question to you is why did you give up on them? No one, no obstacle, or demon in hell can stop you from reaching that milestone. Do not allow yourself to stop you from reaching the peak of the mountain. You do not have to stay in your current situation. You can always choose to keep going. If you choose to stay in the situation, you will not accomplish the milestones that you want to reach. So why stay stuck in a situation that you can get out of? It is time to work towards the goals and conquer the milestone that is in front of you.

Perspective

At times we may not understand the quiet parts of life or as some would say, the calm parts of life. But it is in the calm parts that we can learn the most lessons. Whether you like it or not, things like this will occur. Take those moments and make the best of it. We all deal with shortcomings, but there is always better too if you keep going. Just like a plant that grows over time, we as people will grow over time as we go through this thing called life. In the growing stages you go through each emotion. You will experience happiness, sadness, anger, and frustration. During all those emotions and the calm seasons of life, growth is still happening. Always understand that in calmness there are still remarkable things happening. So do not rush, take your time because the best is yet to come.

Foundation

In order to build something sturdy it is important to have a solid and good foundation. A good foundation does not have cracks. It is not lopsided, nor is it made of cheap material. A solid foundation is built with love, compassion, durable material and is leveled out correctly. When building things with her spiritually, mentally emotionally, and naturally make sure the foundation has been built correctly. If you do not know how to build your foundation, seek God and He will direct your steps. If we are built on Him, everything else will fall in place because He is our firm foundation. While building, there may be obstacles and shortcomings. Continue to build and not worry about what is thrown your way because if you build it on the firm foundation, it will not move.

Beauty

B: Blessed to be on the other side of bondage which is freedom.

E: Every chance I get I will always give You the honor that is due to Your name.

A: Attempting to fix myself did not destroy the perfect thing that You created. You did not allow it too.

U: Unfortunately, even with my attempts, I could not fix myself.

T: Thank you.

Y: You fixed me up and made me look brand new again from the inside out.

Secret & Silence

Silencing the things that cause us pain on the inside just destroys us. Do not allow this to happen to you. Silence is a deadly disease that could cause you to be mentally drained. Find someone you are comfortable talking to that you can trust your secrets with. We all go through a period where we silence our secrets. Do not allow the bondage of silence to keep you from healing. Release the things that you have bottled up so that you can walk in your deliverance. Being healed is not easy, it will take determination, maybe a few tears and even separation, but it is achievable.

What are your silent secrets and what needs to be done to help you be free from them?

Obsession and Opportunity

O: Obedience is

B: Better than a

S: Sacrifice

E: Everyone has heard that

S: Signature

S: Saying, before but how

I: Important is it really for

O: Our lives?

N: Nevertheless

O: Obeying

P: Practical

P: Principals you will

O: Obtain

R: Readiness

T: That

U: Unifies the

N: Necessary

I: Intelligence

T: That

Y: You will need to excel in life.

Life

Life has a way of teaching us through lessons. As we learn the lessons of life our endurance for things becomes stronger. Instead of looking at life through the perspective of disaster we must look at it through the perspective of opportunity. Everything we go through in life is because we made a choice. We cannot blame anyone for some of the things that have happened in our lives. We can be dealt a hard hand of cards, but it is up to us to make something out of it. Going through things is inevitable but we were all given a community of people to help us through them. Everything works together for our good and we must remember that no matter how hard life gets, whether it be good or bad. In the process, give yourself room to make mistakes but do not allow your mistakes to make you. We all have a choice that we can make; to make the good or bad out of the situation. What will be your choice? I choose happiness, long life, good decisions, and peace. Do yourself a favor and take a moment to breathe, it will help.

Dark Shadow

It is impossible to run from our shadows but here we are trying to run from what follows us. We run from what is stuck with us because we do not like what it may be. To disconnect from our dark shadows, we must be consumed by light. Where there is light there is no darkness. What have you ran from that can only be overtaken by light? We can also find ourselves running behind the shadows of others because they were our example. Is the shadow you have been following making or breaking you? If it is breaking you, then you must disconnect from that. How can we know who we truly are if we continue to follow behind the shadows of other people?

Sweet Memories

On September 18, 1989, we buried my father with full Military Honors. The Soldiers were in their uniforms holding the riffle and the casket was covered with the United States of America Flag. The pallbearers were also dressed in their uniforms. The unforgettable moment was when the cannonball and rifle released fire three times. My mom, sister, and brother were all trying to deal with the tragic event in their own way. The loss of our father was hard on everyone. Our lives were changed tremendously since this took place. Our father was the missing puzzle piece, and we could never put the puzzle together again. I remember growing up in Jefferson County with my family. It was not easy, but we had some sweet memories there. Behind our single-family home we have every vegetable in our family garden of which you could think. Everything from squash, cucumbers, carrots and even onions. The garden was our way of escape from the "real world." While in the garden there was a sense of peace and laughter even when the stray animals would come for a midday snack. My father would feed the cats and dogs the vegetables that worms may have eaten from. His motto was "what a worm eats is the stray animals treats." As you all may know life can become hard even being with family, but you must find peace within the hardship. What does your peace look like? My peace was being able to make my own decisions and climbing the big apple tree in our front yard. Other than sneaking away with friends, climbing the apple tree was also one of my weekly routines to get away from being on punishment.

Setbacks

Setbacks are not always horrible. They can teach us how to overcome the next thing we encounter. Having a setback in our insecurities can teach us how to become confident in ourselves. Everything is a lesson, and it can help us make a major comeback. I would not be me if I did not experience hardships. They ordered my steps for greatness. One day you will say enough is enough and take the steps to let go of that thing(s) that is causing you to never move forward. Accept the new opportunities that will help you overcome your setbacks. The comeback with be so great that you will not even be phased by the setback. It will be like water under the bridge that you can look back on and say, "that was not so bad after all." Whenever you are faced with a setback, start to encourage yourself and look on the bright side of the situation. For every setback, there shall be a major comeback.

Countless Memories

There will always be good and dreadful things that happen in our lives on which we can reminisce. When remembering what went on in our lives, it will either show us what we should have changed or what we should have left the same. Do not allow what you remember to paralyze you from trying something new. Memories stay the same, but the future can always change. How your future turns out is left up to you. Be brave, astute, kind, bold, patient, understanding, controlled, and honest. Your reputation now will speak for you in the future.

Protect My Heart

I Fell in Love with You. You Captivate
My Heart. The Smile You Bring Can
Light Up a Room from a Distance. Your Divine
Masculinity Carries My Sorrow and the Weight of
My Pain. I Didn't Even ask You to Take on the
Assignment. You Took It Upon Yourself to be My
Saving Grace. Staying Humble Throughout the
Process to
Watch a Mayflower Grow. I Will
Protect You from My Shame. In All
Essence, Your Caring Heart Soothes Me
Like No Other. From Crying, Stress,
Worrying to Be Myself, I Couldn't Pretend to Be
Something I am Not. Your Love Gave Me Hope and
I Still Have to Protect My Heart.

Titles

Every person's name holds a title. Holding a title is like making everything exist around you clearly. Titles can sometimes change our character. Sometimes it is not just to be famous or to be noticed. Have your name in the spotlight to be recognized. Could you be happy with the money you accumulated? Will you be known for your name or your title? Still, even though you are making a good amount of money, you are still unhappy because you feel empty. Money is essential to get through life. You may have fallen in love with your title. However, just be uniquely you in your own way. The greatest thing you can do is to be yourself without pretending to be somebody else.

Beautiful Kiss

A beautiful kiss as she second-guessed herself, thinking repeatedly, knowing the kiss could not be done. She saw her world, but she would rather for it to stay empty-handed. Riding throughout life protecting her Knight and Shining Armor from dusk to dawn. It could never be one love. Unconditional love was not like anything she had ever experienced in her life. Pure Love was a Blessing and Curse. It became a soul connection between the two. The soul bond of Divine Femininity and not destroying Divine Masculinity showed compassion toward her imperfection. The Twin Flames journey can turn into an out-of-control downward spiral. What is the point of bringing destruction to her first love, Prince

Charming? Do not rescue me, save your good name. I will rescue myself in total darkness. The light throughout the tunnel of universal love. You fought for me when I did not ask you to. Man of honor I will fight for you from a distance. I will always be gracefully sealed with a beautiful kiss. It is an everlasting fantasy of walking through redemption.

True Love

True Love is being true to yourself and remaining true throughout the process of finding yourself in all areas of your life. Know what you want out of life.

Rose

A beautiful soul that was contaminated with thorns from a rose bush in her life. Not being so innocent once the rose petals fell one by one was a tragic identity event. Carrying the sorrow of pain and passion throughout the many waterfalls of sparkling water. Rushing throughout life trying to play catchup knowing it is not anything you need to catch up on. A beautiful multiple colored rose is your true color of divine intention. The reality of life is just a fairytale. You can have anything your heart desires, but you cannot have everything your spirit wants you to have. Falling in love with a deeper spiritual connection to include compassion and understanding.

Raw & Rare

Raw Kindness for Weakness

Raw Imperfection

Raw Accountability

Raw Natural

Raw Bama/ Metro

Rare Transition

Rare Transformation

Rare Transparent

Rare Tranquility

Rare Transpired

Love

Love gives you a Green Light.

Love can give you a Red Light if your character is being deceived.

Love can give you the Yellow Light to precede with caution. It is your identity.

Love is a Narrow Two-way Street.

Love is like a Four-way Stop Sign to see who wants to go first.

Love can be at a Stop Sign, do not go.

Love is a U-turn. Have you learned your lesson?

Love can be a Do Not Enter protect yourself. You are going the wrong way.

Love is not walking into anyone else's union.

Love can come to a Dead End.

Love is No Right or Left Turn, go straight ahead.

Love is the Speed Limit. Do not go fast, watch your speed.

Love is a merge onto the Slippy Road.

Love is a Detour. That was not the person for you anymore.

LOVE IS A PARKING LOT. I HAVE
TO WAIT ON GOD IF I'M GOING TO
GET ANYTHING RIGHT IN MY
LIFE.